A

TREATISE

ON

FRESCO, ENCAUSTIC, AND TEMPERA PAINTING;

BEING THE

SUBSTANCE OF LECTURES

DELIVERED AT

THE SOCIETY OF BRITISH ARTISTS,

AND AT THE

SCHOOL OF DESIGN, LEICESTER SQUARE,

IN THE YEARS 1838-39-40.

By EUGENIO LATILLA,

MEM. SOC. BRIT. ART.

British Library Cataloguing-in-Publication Data
A catalogue record for this book is available from
the British Library

PREFACE.

Many have been the struggles of unaided genius in this country, to sow the seeds of pure taste and sound judgment in the fine arts, even at the sacrifice of private interest, and in opposition to the full tide of prejudice and discouragement. Barry, Fuseli, Flaxman, Stothard, and Hilton, are examples of this; and though their conceptions would have adorned any age, they were suffered to pass through life without a single national commission, or any work of sufficient scope to elicit fully the high powers they possessed.

Public and private bodies have likewise exerted their influence in cultivating a love and just appreciation of the ebullitions of intellect; but to little purpose are institutions formed, or even premiums awarded, where there is not patronage for that character or class of art that can alone dignify a nation, or be profitable to its manufactures.

A more general desire, however, is at length awakened to vie with, and rival other lands that have acquired fame and wealth by their works; and the most effectual means of establishing the arts in their highest principles and pretensions has, at length, been resorted to, in the appointment of a Commission to introduce into England the masterly practice that is raising into fame the schools of Germany and France, namely—Fresco Painting; a medium justly characterized by Fuseli as "the real instrument of history," and which Vasari describes as "truly the most virile, most sure, most resolute, and most durable of all modes."*

The admirable project of embellishing the New Houses of Parliament in fresco is an event, therefore, that will be hailed by all lovers of high art as the means, if judiciously conducted, of exalting British genius, and adding increased lustre to the British name.

In the evidence before the Committee of the House of Commons appointed to take into consideration the promotion of the fine arts in con-

* "Veramente il più virile, più sicuro, più risoluto, e durabile, di tutte gli altri modi."

nection with the rebuilding of the Houses of Parliament, much valuable theoretical information was elicited from artists and amateurs as to the advantages of fresco, and its suitability to large works. Throughout the whole evidence, however, such a total absence of practical knowledge on the subject was evinced, that I have been induced, having for many years made fresco and mural adornment matters of study, research, and experiment, to bring before the public the following "Treatise on Fresco and Encaustic Painting," wherein are detailed the modes practised by the Greeks and Romans, and those of the Italians under the enlightened patronage of Giulio II. and Leo X., with the various stuccoes, colours, mediums, and methods of applying them; also the manner of making Cartoons in Tempera,* a process indispensable to painting successfully *al fresco.*

In this treatise I have endeavoured to obviate the difficulties which present themselves to artists unacquainted with the different modes, in order that the student of history may be induced and urged to attempt the master tones of fresco, or the rich impasto of encaustic, at a period when the

* In a note to Chap. V. I have mentioned an improvement of my own, upon the old method of painting cartoons, which will be found a valuable addition, as it gives the artist nearly the facilities of oil, in scumbling and blending his tints.

Legislature has wisely resolved on introducing mural embellishment upon a grand scale.

On the minutes of evidence I would make a few remarks, as it contains statements that may mislead or convey erroneous notions of fresco.

An artist explained, that fresco was painting with transparent or glazing colours, though the effect, when dry, was that of being solid. This, I beg to say, is not the case; for transparent colour on the stucco will appear so, in the same way as painting with transparent colour on white paper. It is true that the Greeks occasionally made slight decorative figures in this manner, but all the grand subjects, both by the Greeks and Italians, were in a powerful impasto, as are the frescoes of the Vatican.*

Some years ago, I painted a Bacchante in fresco with transparent colour for — Thellusson, Esq., which, of course, was equally transparent when dry; but this style does not bear comparison with the Greek or Italian stucco solidly painted.

The frescoes (so called) in the Roman Catholic chapel at Moorfields, and the Town Hall at Manchester, were referred to in the evidence as failures;

* I have some frescoes by Paul Veronese, in which also, the impasto is very powerful.

but no one explained why they were so. I, therefore, take this occasion to expose an imposition, probably the result of ignorance, practised in both instances, which has operated injuriously to the introduction of fresco in other parts of the country. Having closely examined these paintings, particularly those at Manchester, I perceived them to be not genuine fresco, but what the Italians term mezzo-fresco; which is beginning upon a large surface of wet plaster, and finishing with tempera, &c., though the pictures at Manchester are finished with oil, or varnish colours. This method is well known by painters in fresco to be extremely perishable. Vasari describes it as "the most short-lived," and "the retouches," says he, "soon turn black;" which has been precisely the case with those at the Town Hall, in addition to which the colours are scaling off in many parts.

It was remarked by another artist, that from cartoons the general powers of a painter cannot be known. According to the common idea of cartoons, I grant it would be difficult to judge of them, but not so with those painted in the manner of Raffaelle or Julio Romano, in which the highest powers can be exercised. Cartoons, the size of the intended pictures, would alone enable the

Commission to judge of the abilities of the artists, and he who shewed himself incapable of making large cartoons, would be found still more incapable of painting large frescoes. Many can design subjects admirably in small, who would be utterly at a loss in works of magnitude; for which reason small designs should be disregarded. Large cartoons, by various artists, could be exhibited at once in the situations they were intended to occupy, when the fitness and harmony of the whole would be seen; besides which, cartoon painting is the best possible preparatory study for fresco.

Respecting the subject of competition, there appeared much difference of opinion in the evidence, yet it is no doubt the most just, as well as the most certain course to bring to light the real talent of the country.* It is true that some of those who enjoy the sway in art, though following perhaps some minor branch of it, will not be disposed to compete in a work of a high class, where probably the zeal and ambition of younger aspirants might eclipse their efforts; for many, condemned at pre-

* The first cupola of modern times, at Florence, by Brunelleschi, and the splendid bronze doors of the Baptistry, by Lorenzo Ghiberti, when he was only twenty years of age, were the happy results of competition, not, as is too often the case with us, for cheapness, but excellence.

sent to uncongenial employment, thirst for the higher scope that a national work can alone afford them.

For carrying into effect the establishment of a British School of Fresco, opportunities for the exercise and trial of artists should be given in some public building, as Westminster Hall, according to Mr. Barry's suggestion, for which, cartoons in tempera of the proper size should be required. The designs selected might then be executed in fresco, and compensatory premiums adjudged; first, for the successful cartoons, and secondly, for the frescoes which are painted from them. Thus, an interesting monument of the first essay of British skill in fresco, would be obtained and preserved, at a moderate expense.

About thirty-five years ago there were some fresco and encaustic pictures painted in this country by Rigaud. Those at Packington in Warwickshire I have not seen, but understand them to be in excellent condition. The encaustic ceiling of the Court Room of Trinity House, which consists principally of groups of cherubs, is in a fine state of preservation. It has not turned black like oil, neither is it cracked, which in England is considered, though without foundation, a certain concomitant of encaustic.* The Greeks, on the contrary, looked upon it as the most enduring, and the specimens extant prove the justness of their opinion.†

The only recent attempt at encaustic of which I am aware, is that of the Banqueting Room of His Grace the Duke of Beaufort, at Beaufort House, painted by myself. This encaustic is one of my own discovery, and resembles fresco in effect, with rather more depth of colour, and admitting a higher finish. The design throughout is original, though in Greek taste. The single figures in the large panels were not, as has been supposed, taken from Herculaneum, but nature, as also the fruits and flowers in the arabesques. The character of the composition being bacchanalian, scrolls of the acanthus, with boys and panthers, the size of life, are introduced in the cove. The ornaments, drawn and executed by assistants, may rank among the most masterly specimens ever produced in this country; they are drawn in a grand

* It is generally thought that the pictures of Sir Joshua Reynolds have cracked owing to their being painted with a portion of wax, though it is entirely attributable to his too free use of Venice turpentine.

† I have in my possession an encaustic picture from Pompeii, which is still perfect in colour, and entirely free from cracks.

gusto, and painted in a vigorous impasto, strongly resembling the style of Giovanni da Udine, the very reverse of the method pursued under the direction of house-painters and upholsterers, which is a system of japanning, or tea-tray painting, by no means artistic. I speak thus with freedom of a part of the work not by my own pencil, in justice to those who, by their exertions in a work of a high class, proved themselves equal to any thing that may be required in the way of ornament, thereby entirely subverting the evidence taken before a former Committee, where it was represented as necessary to send to France, both for designers and painters of arabesques.

In the various mouldings of the cornice and stucco ornaments, I applied the Greek principle of colour to an extent that in description might alarm, though, as a whole, it has received the approbation of many of the first artists and men of taste.

This room was to have been painted by Germans; and the idea had so possessed men's minds that English artists were unfit for a work of the kind, that the public papers ascribed it to them. Though much desire appeared on the part of some of the members of the Committee that Cornelius, or some other German artists, should be employed for the new Houses of Parliament, yet it is to be hoped that the present Commission will be more just, as well as more patriotic, and first prove that Englishmen have failed, before they invite a foreigner, unless it be to take a part with the rest of the competitors.

That talent is not wanting is evident, by the superlative excellence attained in those branches that receive support; and equal success would most probably follow the encouragement of the higher grades. The national glory depends greatly on its intellectual contributors, and original productions in poetry, painting, sculpture, and architecture, form lasting sources of revenue, that requite the outlay of the State a thousand-fold.

If the Legislature considers the nation's honour and advantage in this matter, Englishmen will adorn the Senate Houses where Englishmen legislate, and they will exert their energies to compete, not only with Germany and France, but Rome herself.

CONTENTS.

CHAPTER VII.

CHAPTER VIII.

CHAPTER IX.

CHAPTER X.

CHAPTER XI.

ON

FRESCO PAINTING.

CHAPTER I.

ON THE RISE AND PROGRESS OF ART AMONG THE GREEKS, AND THE INTRODUCTION OF FRESCO AND ENCAUSTIC PAINTING.

"SUCH is the influence of the plastic arts on society, on manners, sentiments, the commodities and the ornaments of life, that we think ourselves generally entitled to form our estimate of times and nations by its standard. As our homage attends those whose patronage reared them to a state of efflorescence, or maturity, so we pass with neglect, or pursue with contempt, the age or race which want of culture or of opportunity averted from developing symptoms of a similar attachment."

Thus said that genius, philosopher, and scholar, Fuseli, and the enlightened part of mankind concur in the sentiment. Poets and historians record emphatically the brilliant eras of Pericles, Augustus, and Leo X., while ignominious silence, like night, shades many an intervening period.

High art has by all great nations, ancient and modern, been esteemed a basis and medium for promoting civilization and refinement. Where it is zealously cultivated, an empire assumes in its character the distinctive marks of intellectual superiority and power; while the ebullitions of genius in depictive poesy, which disseminate taste and knowledge, upon high principles, through the various ramifications of society, cannot fail giving to commerce value, to industry an impetus, and to human nature added dignity.

It is not to the honour of a people to continue in a state of partial civilization; neither can the excursive mind of man rest satisfied in seeking merely the necessaries for subsistence, or even the enjoyment and gratification of sense. Such a state, though somewhat beyond that of the brutes, ill becomes the being who was formed in the Creator's image. Man must always be considered with reference to his intellectual capacities; he contemplates the past, the present, and the future. All things, physical or metaphysical, are objects of his analysis, and he rises superior to the sphere in which he moves; but infinity, space, and the knowledge of that wisdom and power by which all things exist and have their being, shew to man his inferiority, and, without circumscription or boundary to his inquiries, the greatness of Omnipotence is displayed in proportion as his research extends, for the further he penetrates, wider plains for observation present themselves to view; one thing accomplished is but the means of apprehending what is still beyond.

> "Creation widens, vanquished nature yields;
> Her secrets are extorted—art prevails."

That benefit as well as dignity accrue to a nation by the cultivation of the elegant arts is indisputable. There are few to be found in the present day with similar sentiments to the narrow-minded prelate, who declared that a pin-maker was a more valuable member of society than Raffaelle; yet, notwithstanding its increase and superior estimation, art, as an instrument in educating the mind, as well as the eye, is in England but partially understood and acknowledged.

The parent mother knows full well the advantage of little illustrated books in facilitating the first impressions of her offspring; and now that these publications abound, the infant mind is taught to reflect at an earlier period, and is sooner, and with less difficulty, expanded and matured.

But the primer and the child's book are far from being the only ones aided by design; our history and our poetry are adorned and elucidated with scenes from nature and imagination, which exhibit the fact, or assist the illusion.

Our scientific works, also, are rendered lucid and perspicuous by graphic delineation; and intricacies and phenomena are by this means explained, that would otherwise, in the absence of the reality, be ambiguous or unintelligible.

The reader of Homer will best understand the author by reference to Flaxman's outlines, unless he is versed in Greek antiquities and customs.

The beautiful facts of Holy Writ will be the better conceived by an acquaintance with the Cartoons of Raffaelle; instance that of "The Sacrifice at Lystra," where the priest of Jupiter is about to offer the victim to Paul and Barnabas. This scene, with very slight alterations, was taken from a Greek bas-relief (now at Florence), and therefore enables us to form a correct notion of the occurrence.

What should we have known of the Egyptians, their temples, their customs? Of Thebes, with its hundred gates? or the magnificence of Carnac, without the remains of art handed down to us? We should be as ignorant of these as we are respecting Jerusalem, of which, though so much has been written, we possess but very indefinite ideas, since scarcely a monument of its former greatness is preserved, and not even one stone remains upon another.

Of Babylon, again, notwithstanding the records of Herodotus, Strabo, Xenophon, Diodorus, and Josephus, how little do we know! Who can determine or portray with authority (seeing that not a vestige of art remains) its mighty walls, its hanging gardens, or its palaces of unequalled dimensions, which have passed like a tale that is told?

How different to this is our cognizance of Greece! from whence streams of intelligence and information have flowed down to us through her treasures of art. With these impressed on our minds, we familiarly enter into the spirit of the ancient writers; their kings, warriors, statesmen, philosophers, and poets, are all known to us; we are as well acquainted with Pericles and the Cæsars, as with Henry VIII. or Charles I.

Where art is not found conjointly with history and poetry, we are at a loss, after a lapse of years, to comprehend the descriptions, and our conjectures are often as vague as they are vain.

Our ideas of the Olympic games are formed upon the splendid examples of Grecian sculpture; and of the gladiators we have the most accurate representations possible; they themselves, with their extraordinary muscular developments, having served as the models.

Unfortunately, no paintings by Apelles have survived the devastations of the cities which they formerly adorned; but the sculpture of Phidias and Praxiteles have been the grand models of imitation to the present day.

By the principles of science, derived from Hippocrates, Pythagoras, Euclid, and Plato, the Greek painters were led to form a just standard of excellence. They acquired precision and boldness from the knowledge of the construction of the human body, its proportions, the unity of its parts, and the laws of its mechanical evolutions.

The systems of the Greeks were founded upon analysis and synthesis. The doctrines and truths of nature were, during successive ages, unfolded by deep research, and with the advance of science may be traced the rise of art.

It was from the absence of fundamental precepts, demonstrating causes and effects, that painters and sculptors, from the 5th to the 14th century, were unable to infuse dignity or vigour into their works. Compare such mechanical labours with the creations of Phidias! In his Panathenaic frieze, the horses and their riders are in motion; the men are intelligent beings of the finest mould; the chargers are heated with impetuosity, snorting and prancing, instinct with life and energy! The perfection of nature and art united.

In order to examine fresco and encaustic, as introduced by the Greeks, it is necessary to trace briefly the first principles of painting, which, according to Pliny, they derived, with those of sculpture and architecture, from the Egyptians.

Painting was the discovery of Giges; though the well-known legend imputes it to the Corinthian maid, who traced the resemblance of her departing lover by the shadow from a lamp.

The earliest attempt at delineation was the skiagram, or representation of a shadow in black on a light ground. This was drawn with the cestrum, a pointed iron instrument, used as a pen for writing on tablets of wax.

The figures on the most ancient Greek vases, commonly called Etruscan, were probably skiagrams; the figures being entirely black, and badly drawn; very similar to the sculpture of the Dædalean school, and bearing some affinity to the Egyptian hieroglyphics, though with a spirit and animation of style that rendered them greatly superior.

The monogram was the next step in advance.

This was the outline of the figure, with portions of detail.

The third was the monochrom, or painting with a single colour; such probably were the best of the Greek vases, where the figures are relieved by a black or brown back-ground. This process was carried to the utmost perfection, and for drawing, invention, and composition, these monochroms are justly held in the highest estimation.

In each stage the Greeks acquired excellence, till all were perfected by the introduction of the Polychrom, or science of colour; which, in the hands of men already possessed of the grand linear principles, could not fail of being an instrument of power, and of completing the basis of pictorial excellence.

The colours were at first few, and used in an impasto of wax, tempered with oil, while warm. The cestrum was used, not like the graver, as is commonly supposed, but much in the way painters now dexterously handle the spatula; drawing with the point, and regulating the impasto with the side of the instrument.

The first great painter in encaustic was Polygnotus, of whose works lengthened descriptions have been handed down. He was, as far as we can ascertain, the founder of epic painting. The *ποικίλη στοα* derives its name from the various pictures by which he adorned it. These were of a grand monumental character, as "The Siege and Sacking of Troy," "The Battle of Theseus and the Amazons," "The Battle of the Lacedæmonians and Athenians, at Œnoe, in Argolis," "The Triumph of Miltiades and the Victors of Marathon." This last celebrated picture was painted by public desire, and such was the admiration in which it was held, that the Athenians offered to reward the artist with whatever he might desire. Polygnotus nobly declined asking any thing; upon which the Amphictyonic Council proclaimed that he should be maintained at the public expense wherever he went.

A chamber of the Propylæa was adorned entirely with the paintings of Polygnotus; and from the accounts of Pausanias, the Acropolis must have been rich with his conceptions. Two immense pictures are also mentioned as adorning the public Hall at Delphi. Many opinions have been rashly formed in deterioration of these works (probably from the character of the descriptions by Pausanias), which resemble Raffaelle's episodes; that, for instance, of the liberation of Peter from prison, where he is first seen asleep, the angel touching him by the hand, while on one side of the same picture the angel is seen leading him out. The anachronism cannot be commended, yet who does not regard the picture with intense admiration? Greek painting should be judged of by Greek sculpture and architecture, and the splendid works that *are* extant, ought to teach us to judge justly of those that are *not*. It is unreasonable to suppose that the applause of the enlightened Athenians could have been bestowed on paintings inferior to the sculpture of Phidias, who was the contemporary of Polygnotus. But if art does not exist in proof, the eulogiums of poets and historians are scarcely accredited; evidently shewing that we are more indebted to the arts for substantiating our knowledge than we are willing to admit.

Arcesilaus, of Paros, Apollodorus, Parrhasius, Zeuxis, and Aristides, all painted in encaustic with the cestrum. This, however, was soon supplanted by the pencil, in which Apelles, Protogenes, and Timanthus excelled.

Pausias, in restoring some of the pictures of Polygnotus, was reproved for handling weapons not his own, because he had used the pencil on a picture painted with the cestrum. It was probably after the introduction of the pencil, by Apollodorus, that the method of painting in fresco was adopted, though it seems to have been in use at a much earlier period for plain walls of a single colour (the colour being mixed with the stucco), trowelled on, and afterwards polished. Although a very ancient mode of painting, the origin of fresco is involved in obscurity; yet it is probable that the Greeks owed much of their enlargement of practice to this aggrandizing medium. Their love for art was interwoven with all their associations. They gloried in their artists, and these, in return, vied with each other in their endeavours to advance the nation's greatness, while the hope of a crown of laurel gave a further impetus to their genius and their exertions. The poets sung, the philosophers discoursed, and painters and sculptors embodied and perpetuated their conceptions, as well as their deeds and persons.

Taste, derived from art, exhibited itself through the manufactures; and those articles (and they are numerous) which have descended to us, are remarkable for beauty and elegance of form. Furniture, apparel, ornaments, armour, weapons, culinary vessels, and pottery of all descriptions, are the production of a people highly refined; even a common earthenware lamp possesses an air of genuine taste that has never been surpassed. The sword, battle-axe, helmet, and shield, are in numberless instances superb works of art; and when brought into juxtaposition with those of more modern times, the superiority of the Greek manufacture will at once be obvious. There are also admirable monuments extant, in the way of pictorially adorned chambers al fresco, with splendid ceilings: the treatment of subject in which (whether historical or mythological) excites our wonder, as also the disposition of ornament which forms the magnificent framework to the pictures introduced. In the arabesque is seen foliage, bacchanals, centaurs, nymphs, animals, birds, and fishes. These, which if disposed by less skilful hands, would have presented abhorrent incongruities, are here amalgamated so as to create new forms and contrasts, which, in a beauteous harmony of colour, strike and gain upon the beholder, so that the mind and senses are equally enthralled. These exquisite inventions have continued to charm through the various changes of ages and dynasties; and having their foundation in every thing that is perfect in nature, they must ever retain their celebrity; while the consecutive inventions of caprice, prejudice, and fashion, sink into deserved oblivion.

CHAPTER II.

ON THE RISE AND PROGRESS OF ART AMONG THE ITALIANS, AND OF FRESCO PAINTING IN PARTICULAR.

In contemplating a master-piece of art, wrought by an expanded intellect with wonderful manual dexterity, and comprehending science, invention, action, passion, chiaro-scuro, and the magic spell of expression, we gaze with wonder and admiration, and forget that ages were occupied and passed in progressive advances; each generation adding its experience to the past, till, ultimately, some genius, with the power of applying the various points of knowledge attained by many, unites their excellences; and, like the skilful chemist, purging away the drossy incumbrances, presents to the world art in its highest attainable perfection! Thus, what we often look upon as the facile production of a day, cost, in its acquirement, many centuries.

There are many who paint, as there are many who rhyme; but few are destined to outlive the narrow limits of their own existence, or who will be recognized as painters and poets by posterity.

The genius of painting, like that of poetry, though intuitive, must necessarily be cultivated; it is therefore highly important to observe the steps by which art rose, the course of its current, and the circumstances under which it flourished. I may, therefore, be excused, while tracing somewhat of the progress of the Italians, and marking those whose genius, or powers of invention, assisted to raise it to the enviable elevation which it attained in the 16th century, through the powers of fresco painting.

Though the Greeks were never surpassed in form, composition, and colour, yet, from the discovery of the science of perspective in the 15th century, a greater command was given to the Italian painters to represent objects as they really appear in nature, and by such unerring rules as enabled them to avoid the incongruities so apparent in the early Florentine school, and even, at times, in the Greek.

After the fall of the Roman empire, art, literature, and science, as is well known, remained at the lowest ebb for the space of several centuries; the barbarians destroying not only every vestige of art, but also every description of knowledge by which it might be re-established. This period of the world's history is justly denominated the dark ages. Among the degenerated Greeks there were, however, a few Gothic painters deserving of notice. At Florence there is a picture by Andrea Rico, of a Madonna and Child attended by angels, which exhibits considerable talent, and is interesting as one of the best specimens of the 13th century. There is also a Madonna and infant Christ in the church of Santa Maria Maggiore, at Rome, pronounced by the Italian painters and writers to be of the 11th century; though it is venerated as a work of St. Luke by Roman Catholics.

Cimabue, a Florentine, born in 1240, was the first Italian who attempted painting in fresco and tempera. He derived his instructions from the Greek artists who had fled to Florence; and from the progress he made, and the dignity he imparted to his figures, he has been styled the Michael Angelo of his day; though at this early period, when the powers of painting were comparatively unknown, a little sufficed to create astonishment. As an instance of this—the Florentines seeing a picture of a Madonna and Child, with ministering angels, the size of life, by Cimabue, an attempt that had not been made by any artist of the time, such a sensation was created, that a feast was proclaimed throughout the city. The painter and picture were carried in grand procession, and with tumultuous rejoicing, to the church of Santa Maria Novella, heralds sounding their approach. The concourse that followed was immense, and the delight occasioned by the picture was so great, that the place where Cimabue resided was named "Bergo Allegri."* Having resuscitated painting, taught many disciples, and lived in wealth and honour, he died in the year 1300. Cimabue was, undoubtedly, the founder, not only of the Tuscan school, but of modern art. He was succeeded by his pupil Giotto, whose abilities, as painter, sculptor, and architect, deserve high recommendation. Not content with the condition of art as left by his master, he strove assiduously to improve it, which he unquestionably did; especially by the practice of fresco; and was fortunate enough to find patrons, who enabled him to prosecute his designs. He studied nature, and improved his conceptions by an intimacy with Dante, whose lofty imagery tended greatly to enlarge men's minds, and to disperse the darkness that had so long enveloped Europe; it also infused into the works of the painters of the day, and many of those who succeeded, a charm which will ever be acknowledged. Giotto's Belfry at Florence, which still exists, is a

* Vasari.

fine piece of architecture. It is a tower of great height, of inlaid marbles (corresponding to the duomo), and is adorned with sculptured figures that possess beauty and simplicity. This artist was much, and deservedly, esteemed by popes, kings, and princes. It is related of him, that while engaged on a fresco at Porto Reale (the entrance to Naples), the king Ruberto often visited him, and said one day, in conversation, that he intended to make him the first man in the kingdom. "It is for *this* reason, then," answered Giotto smiling, "that I am stationed here!" On another occasion, the weather being very oppressive, the king said, "I would leave painting a little while it is so warm, if I were you, Giotto." "And I certainly would," answered the painter, "if I were your Highness."

From the time of Giotto, the love of art seems to have spread rapidly, and pictures subsequent to this period are to be found in all the principal cities of Italy.

Philip Brunelleschi, the founder of the modern school of architecture, and the restorer of the Tuscan, Doric, Ionic, and Corinthian orders, aided greatly in improving the style both of fresco and sculpture by the necessity he created for works corresponsive to the classic grandeur of his edifices.

He was the discoverer of the mode of erecting

cupolas, which had been lost since the time of the Romans.

Vasari relates a similar anecdote of him to that recorded of Columbus, though this has unquestionably the merit of being the first, since it occurred before the birth of Columbus.*

A council of the most learned men of the day and from various parts of the world, was summoned to consult and shew plans for the erection of a cupola like that of the Pantheon at Rome.† Brunelleschi refused to shew his model, it being upon the most simple principles, but proposed that the man who could make an egg stand upright on a marble base should be the architect. The foreigners and artists agreeing to this, but failing in their attempts, desired Brunelleschi to do it himself: upon which he took the egg, and with a gentle tap broke the end, and placed it on the slab. The learned men unanimously protested that any one else

* Brunelleschi died in 1446; Columbus was born in 1442.

† Some of these wise men proposed that a centre column should support the dome; others, that a huge mound of earth (with quatrini scattered among it) should be raised in the form of a cupola, and the brick or stone work built upon it. When finished, an order was to be issued, allowing the people to possess themselves of what money they might find in the rubbish; the mound would thus be easily removed, and the cupola be left clear.

could do the same; to which the architect replied with a smile, that had they seen his model they could as easily have known how to build a cupola.

The work then devolved upon him, but a want of confidence existing among the operatives and citizens, they pronounced the undertaking to be too great for one man, and arranged that Lorenzo Ghiberti,* an artist of great repute at that time, should be co-architect with him. Brunelleschi's anger and mortification were so great on hearing this decision, that he destroyed, in the space of half an hour, models and designs that had cost him years of labour, and would have quitted Florence but for the persuasions of Donatello.

It is almost unnecessary to add, that the cupola was completed with perfect success by Brunelleschi, since St. Peter's, at Rome, and our own St. Paul's, were formed upon the model of his dome at Florence.

Paolo Uccelli painted in fresco, but was principally absorbed in the study of perspective, and first introduced into painting its invaluable principles. He laboured incessantly, and often spent whole nights in discovering the termination or intersection

* Lorenzo Ghiberti was the sculptor of the exquisite bronze doors of the Baptistry, at Florence, which Michael Angelo admired so much as to say they might serve for the gates of Paradise.

of a line; and like most men who have devoted their minds to occult sciences, he lived in poverty, and died neglected, though it must be acknowledged that he conferred one of the greatest benefits upon art, and posterity has reason to record his name with consideration.*

Piero Francesco was another who devoted himself to perspective; he wrote many volumes on the subject, and has even been styled by some the father of the science; and from the painters of his time beginning to estimate his value, he received more honour and emolument than the unfortunate Uccelli.

Masaccio was a man who likewise advanced his art; he treated history with extraordinary skill, and many of the greatest painters have studied his works in the Brancacio Chapel, Michael Angelo and Raffaelle among the number.

At this time painting both in oil and fresco was, however, practised in a gothic gusto,† and the

* Paolo Uccelli painted a curious picture, which is worth mention, as it correctly classified the artists according to their merit. In it, he represented Giotto as the luminary of modern painting, Brunelleschi of architecture, Donatello of sculpture, himself of perspective, and Giovanni Maneti of mathematics. Paolo painted buildings in perspective.

† While the gothic architecture of the dark ages attained to beauty, which is still justly admired, the same cannot be said of gothic paintings, which, though curious, should never be deemed examples worthy of imitation.

artists of the day were engaged in illustrating scripture for the instruction of the people. Pinturichio was employed to paint the Library of Siena, and called to his assistance Raffaelle, then young in art and reputation, who painted one panel and made designs for the rest. But the fame of Michael Angelo and da Vinci reaching him, he could no longer remain at Siena, but, leaving the walls unfinished, he repaired to Florence. " The Cartoon of Pisa," by Michael Angelo, and " The Battle of the Standard," by Leonardo, speedily made him leave his gothic style, and improve himself on the models of the antique. He was shortly after called upon to paint a stanza in the Vatican, through the interest of his uncle, Bramante, who was designing at St. Peter's, and was in high favour with the Pope.

Many of the rooms were already completed,* but on seeing what had been done, he determined to surpass it all, and to the astonishment of the Pontiff Giulio II., the marvellous composition of " The School of Philosophy"† appeared, like a meteor in the midst of stars of common magnitude. The Pope, doing justice to the splendid talent that had developed itself, immediately ordered all the other

* By Perugino Pietro della Francesca, Luca da Cortona, Bartolomeo della Gatta, and Bramantino da Milano.

† Commonly, but erroneously, called " The School of Athens."

chambers to be defaced, and adorned by the superior genius of Raffaelle.*

Here is an instance of a painter being elevated to his proper dignity through having free scope for the faculties of his mind; though no one anticipated "The School of Philosophy" from Raffaelle, who till that period had only been rather better than his master Perugino.

In his moral frescoes Raffaelle expanded as in a congenial element; he

"Reigns here and revels,"

and exhibits all the rare attributes for which he is distinguished. Form, invention, chiaro-scuro, and even colour, are all excellent in the frescoes of the Vatican. He seemed to have apprehended all that could render art perfect, and what he had witnessed by Buonaroti and Da Vinci in design, enabled him to carry painting to an unprecedented altitude.

His execution was only surpassed by his conception: his line was always energetic, however delicate and beautiful, and of expression, like Aristides the Theban, he has justly been called the master. Truth is stamped on his cartoons, and he vividly recals the events of former days. "The School of

* Out of respect to the work of his master, Raffaelle preserved the ceiling painted by him, which is still to be seen in the Vatican.

Philosophy," "The Dispute of the Sacrament," " The Liberation of Peter from Prison," " The Miracle of Bolsena," and the " Incendio dell Borgo," are the perfection of historic art, and display a concentration of powers entirely his own. His portraits, though few in number, are of the highest order; those of Giulio II. and Leo X. are fine examples.

His Madonnas are the most fascinating personifications of maternal affection, mingled with dignity and grace, the very beau-ideal of female tenderness. That called the Madonna della Seggiola, the gem of the palace that contains it at Florence, is, perhaps, the most perfect and exquisite. Regarding the sculpture and painting of the Greeks, with a keen perception of their well-founded principles, and their high standard of excellence, formed upon the infinitude of Nature, Raffaelle sought with eagerness all that could be collected of Grecian art, and for that purpose sent artists to Greece to copy any thing that was beautiful, and in emulation of the Baths of Titus, he conceived and executed his loggie of the Vatican. What he beheld by the pencil of the Greeks impelled him onward to equal, if not in some respects to surpass, their splendid achievements. The example of Raffaelle was followed by his school, and taste spread through Italy with rapid strides. The revival of pictorial excellence was hailed by all the learned and wealthy of the age: genius created patronage; patronage, in its turn, fostered talent; and Rome, which before had been renowned for the arts of war, then became pre-eminent as the restorer of the arts of peace.

The next great painter in the history and successful practice of fresco who demands our particular attention is Michael Angelo. He was directed by Giulio II., at the instigation of Bramante (who, jealous of his abilities, was anxious that he might be engaged in some work wherein he might fail), to undertake the embellishment of the Sixtine Chapel: although he strongly recommended Raffaelle, as better able to accomplish it than himself, who had never painted in fresco. But his endeavours to evade the commission failed. The Pope, from a perception, probably of his commanding powers, and in order to provoke to excellence in painting the sublimity and grandeur of style so remarkable in his sculpture, insisted on the undertaking. Michael Angelo accordingly drew his cartoons, and obtained some Florentine painters to assist him with the fresco.* But finding their dry, cramped gothic manner subversive of his breadth and flow of outline, he without ceremony destroyed

* Grannacio, Juliano Bugiardino, Jacopo di Sandro, L'Indaio Vecchio, Agnolo di Domino, and Aristotle.

all their labours, and began the tremendous undertaking entirely alone, securing the doors, and not suffering himself to be seen, either at home or at the Capella, while the disgraced Florentines returned with shame to their own city. After indefatigable exertion during several months, he exhibited to view a portion of the most unrivalled ceiling that was ever painted. Sublimely conceived, drawn with a skill that surpassed all previous achievements, it excited the immortal Raffaelle to efforts that rendered him afterwards the successful rival of Michael Angelo.

The Pope, who had been eagerly waiting for a sight of what had been done in the Capella, did not even allow the dust to subside from the removal of the scaffolding, but was the first to enter. A concourse followed, and the most unbounded applause was awarded to the painter. Thus what Bramante hoped would have proved injurious to Buonaroti, served but for his further exaltation, and for Raffaelle's imitation. Success usually attends great minds when incited to vast undertakings, and thus it was with Raffaelle and Michael Angelo. The power or inherent capacity of these men, though undoubtedly far beyond the common order, was unfolded and matured by an enlarged practice, the offspring of splendid patronage, induced be it remembered by the exhibition of *one single essay by each of these artists* in fresco, the noblest of all mediums, and the one most adapted to elicit the latent powers of the pencil.

It was primarily from the *nature* of the practice required in fresco painting, that the grand style of the Italian school arose, and I will venture to affirm, that no school can be high in character or of the first order without the same enlarged means of study. It is to me no matter of surprise that high art is prostrate, while that which dignified the great schools of Italy is thrown aside and contemned. Yet who that has been rapt in admiration at the wonders of the Sixtine Chapel could wish to see the exalted genius of Michael Angelo confined within the narrow limits of a few feet of canvass? But had he lived in these days, men would have been alarmed at the size and strength of his figures, and might probably have advised more caution, more neatness, and more attention to the academic rules. Left, however, unfettered and uncontrolled, he rose above all rules, and, disdaining

——————" To beat
The beaten track,"

he, in a surprising manner, mastered every thing that came within the compass of art, and levelled every barrier that obstructed its advancement.

As sculptor, Buonaroti shewed no less the master mind. The tombs of Lorenzo di Medici and Giulio II. evince both the skill of the painter and architect ; the pictorial effect and architectural arrangement afford a fine example of the union of the three branches. The Moses as a statue is a sublime conception of the Lawgiver, and one of the grandest efforts of the chisel.

As architect, Michael Angelo raised the loftiest dome in Europe, perfect in its proportions, and beautiful in all its parts ; he elevated it a hundred feet beyond the original design, and would have added to the fabric one of the noblest porticoes imaginable, had not death prevented the fulfilment of his intentions. Thus, in his three-fold capacity of painter, sculptor, and architect, he stands alone and unrivalled.

The excellence of the grand style in painting can only be developed when employed upon an enlarged scale. Talent may be visible in the lower, but in the higher are the noble capabilities of the art alone demonstrated. By encountering difficulties, men learn to overcome them, and it is by artists being employed in great undertakings, that works worthy of the nation will be produced.

Were fresco painting encouraged in England, it would at once effect the rise of British art, and call forth powers that now lie dormant, and must continue so, while no scope is afforded for their display. This is unhappily the case with our historical painters, who, after a few vigorous but discouraged attempts, decline in energy, and, driven by disappointment and the prospect of destitution, adopt a style more congenial to common understandings. Thus the highest walk of art is neglected or forsaken, and instead of exalting the public feeling, artists are constrained to pander to the corrupt taste of the times. It is from the broad principles which fresco painting inculcates, that I consider so much benefit will result from its introduction. In this enobling material every faculty is called forth, and in the exercise of it is created a precision of touch and breadth of style that preclude every meaner detail that would lessen the sublimity of the conception, or contract the genius of the artist, whose thought must be intent only on producing a grand and harmonious combination.

In such a practice the powers of a great mind will necessarily increase, as the demand made upon them is urgent, and thus will be matured the bold hand, the correct eye, and the enlightened judgment.

CHAPTER III.

ON FRESCO FOR MURAL DECORATION.

Fresco (so called from its being painted on a prepared stucco while fresh plastered and wet) is the most masterly of all modes for mural adornment. The Greeks introduced it among the Romans, and most of the ancient frescoes and encaustics were the work of the former, as those of Pompeii and Herculaneum. In various parts of Italy, ancient frescoes have been brought to light, and Vasari says, that such was the beauty and freshness of the Baths of Titus when first opened, that Raffaelle and Giovani da Udine, who had come to see them, remained for some time transfixed with amazement.

The sight of these frescoes led at once to the execution of the Loggie, and the magnificent arabesques and ornamental stuccoes, which have been so justly admired. It was from Giovanni's observing the ornaments in stucco and relievo in the Thermæ, that he invented the mode of casting from moulds in the manner of the antique, with calcined marble and marble dust. Until this, castings were made of chalk, lime, and bitumen, boiled together, and poured into the moulds while hot.

Giovanni also adopted the method that Bramante had discovered, of casting architectural mouldings in lime and pozzolana. The relievos and ornaments came out satisfactorily in this manner as to impression, but not sufficiently white. He afterwards succeeded in imitating the antique, by the substitution of marble dust for pozzolana.

Among the advantages of fresco for mural decoration are, the absence of glare, with exceeding purity, and freshness of colour. Fresco, reflecting instead of absorbing light, renders it particularly beautiful by candle-light, though its bland mellowness of tone is at all times very charming.*

By the practice of this admirable mode of painting, the artist will soon lay aside the lesser excellences required in oil, as they would not be called for, and indeed cannot be exercised in it; the firmness of touch and celerity necessary for completing the part prepared for the day, with a constant reference to the effect of the whole, will prove to the painter that more beauty is caused by simple colour,

* The crudity observed in some modern frescoes may be imputed either to the thinness of the plaster, or to the want of harmony in the colouring of the painter.

more grandeur by preserving the flow of outline, the vigour and general character of the subject, than by attending to tints, glazings, and all the intricacies of oil. Local colour should remain unbroken by various hues; and the chiaro-scuro in fresco seems amply to supply the want of variety of tints. To manage fresco well, requires a practice in the large, after which the painter may successfully treat small subjects; but the material is so adapted for an ample area, that its beauty and facility of manipulation are much lost in very circumscribed limits.

In oil there are certain allurements, as transparency, depth, and richness, which, though totally without the grand essentials of art, may please, and form the principal excellence of pictures worthy of commendation. Not so in fresco; knowledge or ignorance here will be obvious: there is no evading anatomy, drawing, and expression; these are indispensable, and on this account fresco is eminently calculated to form great designers.

The principal works of the renowned Italian masters are in fresco, and they, as Reynolds observes, "are justly considered as the greatest efforts of art which the world can boast."

Michael Angelo, Raffaelle, Giulio Romano, Corregio, the three Caracci, Guido, Domenichino, and

Guercino, were all eminent in fresco, and far surpass, in this material, their pictures in oil, simply because the former developed the higher principles. The Germans, in our own times, have advanced through the same practice, and have acquired, within a very few years, fame throughout Europe. They excel in drawing and design, but, which is quite enigmatical, have selected Francia and Perugino for their models, instead of the unaffected grandeur of the Roman school. Still, the adoption of fresco is a happy omen, and cannot fail to enlarge the taste of the Germans. There are, even now, proofs of extraordinary excellence to be seen among them by rising artists, whose genius is overlooked in the present unsound gusto founded upon early art.

For large mural works, the palm must be awarded to fresco by unprejudiced and intelligent minds. The beauty of this medium is so chaste, its tones so purely historic, and so void of any meretricious admixture, that, though its pretensions are not as numerous as oil, its qualities for the grand style are infinitely superior.

CHAPTER IV.

ON ENCAUSTIC FOR MURAL DECORATION.

THIS is one of the most ancient methods of painting recorded by the Greeks, but, from the fact of their disagreement as to its origin (for they impute to different painters its discovery), it would be vain in our time even to assign the period of its introduction: though it might probably have been suggested by the Mordant painting of the Egyptians. It derived its name (ἐνεκαυσε) from the materials being prepared by fire. It was used for tabular and mural works, and combined the lucid properties of fresco with much of the richness of oil, and, like the former, reflected light.

From the speculations on encaustic painting, a variety of modes have been discovered, and partially adopted; but, among conflicting opinions, the real process of the ancients has, in my opinion, been overlooked, and no other of equal value substituted. Count Caylus was one of the most active movers of the research. On a premium being offered by the

Royal Academy of Inscriptions at Paris for an encaustic that should meet with the approbation of that body, several modes were proposed by three candidates, Count Caylus, Cochin, and Bachiliere. Two of the discoveries were approved, but resolved into one, as it was thought that the conjunction would render the medium more perfect. Wax, liquified in water by an infusion of salt of tartar, formed the composition. I have, however, found that this does not thoroughly bind the colours when used in an impasto, and, moreover, requires varnish.

Several experiments have since been tried, such as the following: wax pastiles blended by heat; colours mixed with wax, and used while hot; gum mastic and wax thrown while hot into cold water, and then pulverized, and used with water-colours; this was also secured by the application of heat; gum mastic and wax dissolved in turpentine, and heat applied to unite the whole. Some of these were burnished by passing an ivory palette-knife over the surface; others, by a coat of melted wax, polished afterwards by a piece of linen or silk. But these being wholly inapplicable for large works, I pass on to some observations made by Pliny upon the ancient method.

"It is certain," says he, "that there were anciently two ways of painting in the encaustic style —on tablets of wax, and on ivory, with the cestrum or engraver's burin. When vessels began to be painted, a third method was adopted, that of melting wax by fire, and laying it on with a pencil; a kind of painting that will bear exposure to the sun, and stand the action of salt-water and the wind without injury."*

Of encaustic *varnish*, as applied to walls painted in fresco, with the colour of minium (or vermilion) Pliny says, "When the wall is well dried, let the best punic wax, liquified with oil and in a heated state, be laid on with a hog's-hair brush; then let it be heated a second time, by applying blackened or charred gall-nuts till the wax begins to melt; afterwards let it be reduced to the proper consistency by means of candles."†

From these rather vague directions, together with observations and experiments of my own, I am induced to think that the medium for *painting* was

* "Encausto pingendi duo fuisse antiquitus genera constat, cera, et in ebore, cestro, id est viriculo, donec classes pingi cuepere. Hoc tertiam accessit resolutis igni ceris penicillo utendi, quae pictura in navibus nec sole, nec sale, ventisque corrumpitur."—Plin. lib. 35.

† "Parieti siccato, cera punica cum oleo liquefacta candens setis inducatur; iterumque, admotis Gallae carbonibus, inuratur usque ad sudorem postea candclis subigatur."—Plin. lib. 35.

the same as Pliny so minutely describes for the varnish; and, though he only mentions wax, it may be in the way we speak of painting in oil, which is not oil alone, though any one ignorant of the process might easily suppose this to be the case, from no other ingredient being named. Wax, alone, suddenly chills, and offers no facility whatever for the pencil. It is true, Lanzi gives an account of a Florentine painter who used colours mixed with wax heated over a fire, the canvass also being heated by another fire at the back; but this could not have been the system of the Greeks, whose encaustics were on walls as well as tablets. Wax tempered with oil, I conceive, therefore, to be the medium; this works easily in an impasto, and produces an exact imitation of the ancient encaustic. The colours were ground with the wax, on a heated stone, as represented in a picture at Pompeii, where the attendant of an artist in the studio is grinding colours on a slab with a fire under it.

Almost every colour was employed in encaustic, as orpiment, red-lead, and other evanescent colours: wax having the property of preserving them from the action of light, and atmospherical changes. The oil when used with wax should be colourless, and a powerful drier. Nut-oil with wax is not easily dried.

The durability of the Greek encaustic must have been great, as it resisted the sun's rays, the wind, and the salt of the sea.

Having long been desirous of seeing fresco and encaustic introduced into England, I have made experiments in the hope of discovering a medium combining the qualities of the two—the freshness, and luminous brilliancy and absence of glare in the former, with the richness and facility of painting in the latter: in this I have at length succeeded beyond my expectations, and shall be glad of an opportunity of displaying its powers to the public.

After having bestowed much time and pains upon this encaustic, I cannot be expected, in justice to myself, to make known advantages which the ancient with all its excellence did not possess, inasmuch as varnish was an essential part of its process. It was in my encaustic, but which has since been greatly improved in richness and durability, that I painted the banquetting-room of His Grace the Duke of Beaufort, and it being without any varnish, the effect of the whole can be seen at once. From the subsequent additions, my encaustic now approximates nearer, in practice and appearance, to fresco, though admitting of a higher finish: it is particularly suitable for works that are exposed to minute observation.

CHAPTER V.

ON TEMPERA.

TEMPERA is the most ancient of all the modes of painting, and was common among the Egyptians, as may be seen in their antiquities preserved at the British Museum. From them, it was doubtless brought into use among the Greeks, to whom the tempera paintings at Pompeii are imputed.

The scenery for the Greek drama may have been painted in the aquazzo, or common size, which Vitruvius mentions as in ordinary use for dry stuccoes.

From occasional remarks by the ancient writers, I am led to think that pictures were sometimes painted in a description of tempera, and varnished. The story of the sponge thrown against a picture by Protogenes, and producing the effect of foam on the horse's mouth, appears to favour the supposition; and the brown harmonizing varnish of Apelles may have been the encaustic varnish used over an exquisite kind of tempera, in the same manner as over fresco, for the preservation of minium.

In the first ages of Christianity, tempera was much practised by Greek painters, whose medium was very powerful and brilliant, as is obvious from many of their works still extant in various parts of Italy.

During the dark ages, tempera, afterwards varnished, seems to have been almost the only mode of painting. The gallery at Florence contains some early Greek pictures of this description, which are of interest from their being in the style that was first imitated by the Italians on the revival of art by Cimabue and Giotto. Considerable excellence was acquired in this medium by the early masters, but it attained its great elevation in the Cartoons of Raffaelle.

The Greek medium and manner of applying it, as afterwards learnt by the Italians, is detailed by Vasari, and is as follows:—

Rosso di uovo (yolk of egg) is beaten up with some of the milky juice that issues from the tender twigs of the fig-tree. The colours having been ground in water, are used with this mixture. Gum water is necessary for occasional glazings. In painting blue draperies, size is better than yolk of egg, as the latter is apt to tinge the blue.

Juice from the fig-tree could not easily be obtained in England, neither is it essential in my opinion.* I have used yolk of egg beaten up with water, and it answers admirably, provided parchment size and a little drying oil are mixed with the white. This tempera possesses the valuable property of retaining its colour the same as when first laid on; which is the case with no other.†

The usual kind of tempera looks very meagre when dry, and becomes considerably lighter; besides which, it does not admit of repeated touchings. The uovo medium will receive high finish, and may be either employed opaquely, or semi-transparently.

In the Colonna Palace at Rome, there are several fine landscapes by Gasper Poussin, à uovo; and in the different collections throughout Europe, tempera pictures may be found, which have been painted as designs for fresco.

* Spurge, or wart-wort, contains a like juice, but a little pale drying oil beaten up with the white and yolk of an egg, forms an excellent medium.

† Tempera à uovo was formerly used in the English cathedrals and churches, introduced, no doubt, by Italians who have been employed in this country. Those paintings called frescoes I have generally found upon examination to be tempera on dry stucco. The colouring on mouldings and capitals has often been in size tempera.

ON PAINTING CARTOONS.

The most important part of the preparation for fresco with which the artist has to do is the cartoon. On this much labour and study must be bestowed; the composition, the drawing, the chiaroscuro, and colour, should all be perfectly considered and well defined before the wet stucco is ventured upon.

For a cartoon, paper is strained or pasted on a frame, covered with lining canvass; if required to be very strong, two layers of paper are necessary, each pasted firmly on. This done, the design is sketched in from a small previous study, with charcoal in a large port crayon, attached to a stick of tolerable length, so as to enable the painter to see the effect of his lines.

The invention designed, and the composition arranged, the drawing must be carefully wrought from models, draperies, &c. It was the custom (and a most valuable one) of the old masters to model their figures in wax, or clay, and to arrange draperies on them composed of linen, or muslin, saturated in clay water. Such figures being disposed in groups on a plane, all the incidental effects of light and shade are perceived and studied, and may then be copied in conjunction with living models.

We know that all the greatest painters adopted a similar method, and it was by means of such that Correggio painted his wonderful foreshortened figures in the Cupola of Parma, in which he was assisted by Begarelli. Raffaelle also pursued the same plan for his principal subjects. In modelling, the painter will give his undivided attention to drawing and composition, apart from the seductions of colour, which too frequently lead him from more important considerations; but a picture painted upon the substantial principles I have described, will not fail to reward the artist by its excellence.

Cartoons should be tinted generally over up to the required effect with burnt or raw umber before proceeding with the colours.

Kremnitz, or permanent white, is the best, and the painter will do well to confine himself to the pigments used in fresco, or he will be at a loss when employed on the stucco.

If the cartoon is painted opaquely, it will be easier to imitate and to be copied by assistants.

The colours are ground in water, and the rosso di uovo kept in a dipper on the palette.

White will work pleasantly. and in an impasto, if mixed with parchment size and a little drying oil, and used with the yolk of egg. The mixing of tints must be left to the judgment and custom of the artist, each having a method of his own.

Draperies of bright colours may be painted with white and black, and then glazed with gum-water and colour. The longer the gum-water has been made the less likely it is to shine.

The best way of transferring the cartoon to the stucco is by means of a pounce, in the following manner:—

Trace an outline from the cartoon, lay it on a thick woollen substance, and, with an etching needle, closely perforate its forms. The indentings of the needle at the back may be removed by rubbing them with pumice-stone. When the portion of the outline designed for the day is cut out and placed on the wall, dab and rub it over with charcoal powder,* and on taking away the paper the black dots will form an outline on the stucco.

This, to those unacquainted with it, may appear an intricate process, but it is sooner done than described, and is, in my opinion, preferable to tracing with a point, as the latter leaves visible furrows on the stucco.

* The rubber is made of a strip of flannel, or woollen cloth, rolled hard, and tied tightly round. Care must be taken to keep the surface of the pounce even.

CHAPTER VI.

ON OIL PAINTING FOR MURAL DECORATION.

OIL is the most beautiful and powerful medium ever discovered for tabular pictures of moderate dimensions. The solidity of colour, combined with transparency, rendering it a charming mode of painting; and for small subjects, animals, landscapes, domestic scenes, and portraits, it is unequalled.

To the colourist it is justly valuable, as by it he can indulge in all the magic of tint; hence the preference of it to fresco by the Venetians, who in the latter not only shew feebleness of drawing, but even want of colour.

With the "decadenza" of art, when national dignity faded before the splendour of private individuals, fresco was little used; oil painting prevailed, and easel and cabinet pictures were treasured up, to the exclusion of high art, and almost to its extinction; there has been little, consequently, in the palaces and public buildings of Europe during the last two centuries worthy the appellation of the grand style. In England, De la Fosse, Verio, and Sir James Thornhill, are commonly considered painters of great classic works, but their style cannot be too much reprobated, even when carried to its utmost excellence in the talent and resplendency of Rubens. The paintings of these men, and the sculpture of Bernini, exhibit a meretricious display of material, and a lamentable prostitution of the grand elements of art. Peruked and Romanized English gentlemen, shepherdesses in hoops and toupees, were the climax of this subversion of taste. Epic painting, especially when mural, suffers and is degraded by the dazzle of roseate and flowery hues, the collision of tints, and the distraction of incompatible objects.

The richness of oil, as seen on a small scale, becomes black, ponderous, and unintelligible on an extensive area. The ceiling, by Rubens, at Whitehall is an example of this; the effect originally was, no doubt, clear and discernible, but it is so no longer. Age, which gives richness to moderate-sized works, causes ultimate obscurity in those that are very large. In the course of a few years, the decorations of the Louvre, though painted light, will inevitably become heavy.

The glare of varnish is another great and insuperable obstruction to the beauty of mural oil painting.

Portions only can be seen at one time, and these at certain angles of vision, and thus the sublimity of a subject is destroyed. Oil colour is also subversive of architectural grandeur, and by artificial light it is dark and gloomy.

The best works on a large scale not in fresco, or encaustic, are those of Paul Veronese, but he painted often in a fine description of tempera, glazed in oil. "The Marriage Feast at Cana of Galilee," at Paris, and a compartment of a ceiling, at Versailles, are examples of this kind; they have all the clearness of tempera, and the richness of oil, without its blackness. This master's works, therefore, possess a superiority over oleaginous pictures generally.*

Oil painting is no more calculated for mural decoration than fresco is for tabular or easel pictures. Each mode possesses intrinsic excellence, and is admirable in its respective and legitimate sphere. The misappropriation of method and style engenders corrupt taste, and superinduces the most incongruous absurdities.

* I have seen a fine luminous sky, by Paul Veronese, come partly away on the application of the sponge and water after the varnish was removed; the picture gave sufficient proof of not being entirely in oil, but it was probably used in conjunction with tempera, the old masters having possessed great skill in the latter medium.

CHAPTER VII.

ON DESIGN FOR FRESCO.

In all large works, great skill and judgment are required in the adaptation of subject, ornament, and general design.

Drawings and models of works in miniature frequently look very agreeable to the eye, which, when magnified and executed, disappoint expectation, the grand object of a design having often been entirely overlooked in the alluring appearance of a drawing in colour and perspective. Design, in its highest consideration, should alone occupy the attention of those who have to decide on such matters.

A simple arrangement of ornament, so as to unite the sequence of historic or epic subjects, is essential to the general effect, and the artist should, as architect and sculptor, as well as painter, consider the disposition of separate parts. The great mural painters combined the three-fold power, and thus acquired a superiority in arranging extensive works, which the simple practice of one of them does not afford. In modern times, sculptors, and architects in general, have little regard for what is pictorial, and painters are not at all interested in what is architectural; and while the Italian rose in the united strength of the three, the artist of this day thinks nothing is to be derived from any branch but the one he owns.

As sculptor, Michael Angelo knew the importance of a single figure, and as architect, where to appropriate it to the utmost advantage.

The ceiling of the Capella Sistina may be regarded as the standard of excellence in this as well as in every other respect. The grand periods of theology are supported, as it were, by the prophetic pillars of sacred writ which form the sublime framework.

Michael Angelo was the only painter who scorned to avail himself of the beauty of ornament. The human form was used by him as the highest style of ornament (which it undoubtedly is); and though the figures are of colossean stature, the ceiling seems to recede, and simplicity as well as grandeur reigns throughout.

The Dome of Parma is another striking example. "The Assumption of the Virgin" is, in its style, pure and dignified; the apostles standing on the cornice, and the patron saints of the city, in the spacious niches of the angles, are majestic personations, and shew consummate skill in arrangement and composition.

The Farnesina, the Farnese, and Rospiglioso palaces, present good examples of the dispositions of groups and single figures in designs for ceilings.

The judicious disposition of subjects on the walls of a building is highly necessary to the beauty of the whole. A succession of large compartments should be relieved by pilasters or ornament. If paintings are too close to each other, the eye has no relief, and one is injurious to the next. Where there is sufficient space, the compositions can hardly be too large, the grandeur being greatly heightened by the size, as in "The Hall of Constantine." The chaste personifications of "Justice" and "Benignity" are fine contrasts to the tumult of "The Battle of Constantine and Maxentius." Large historical pictures in fresco or encaustic should occupy the centres of a spacious apartment, smaller ones may then be disposed to advantage; but a number of small ones diminish apparently the size of a room.

Reference must always be made to the manner of lighting. If light comes from both sides, the beauty of decoration will be much injured, though architects do not sufficiently consider this. If windows are on one side, they should be large, that the light may be well diffused; in this manner the advantage of a painted ceiling may be secured; but the best light is unquestionably from above, as in the Tribune at Florence, the Sculpture Gallery in the Vatican, and the new Grand Gallery at Versailles. In these, uniformity of arrangement is preserved, and they are admirably suited for decoration.

The Stanzas of Raffaelle are very badly lighted, and only frescoes could be seen in them. The Capella Sixtina is insufficiently lighted, and the windows are a disfigurement; under them is a series of pictures, following in too close a succession, by Perugino, Rosselli, and others, whose pigmy efforts contrast strangely with the breadth of the ceiling, and the colossal altar-piece of the "Last Judgment."

Vaulted and coved ceilings are the best for decoration generally; flat ones are rarely beautiful when of great expanse.

For corridors, fine examples may be found in the Baths of Titus; where arabesques, with medallions of historic and poetical subjects, are interspersed. The long gallery of the Vatican that contains the tapestries from the Cartoons, has an exceedingly elegant effect from the skilful disposition of ornament. There are numerous precedents in Italy of decorated corridors that exhibit every variety of ornament, on which artists of all classes seem to have been employed, as in the Loggie.

Men accustomed to this kind of work, as I have found by experience, are soon able to proceed with expedition, and acquire great freedom of touch, on which the beauty of ornament mainly depends. The Acanthus scroll, for instance, derives a peculiar excellence from the colour, being, as it were, modelled by the pencil: this is exemplified in the frescoes of Giovanni da Udine, which are the best in this branch of art.

In designing for fresco and encaustic, only the Greek and great Italian masters should be referred to, for after these, there remain but corrupt examples, some better, some worse, till sublimity is entirely lost in the tumultuous confusion of Pietro da Cortona and his disciples, whose decorations of churches resemble the fantastic scenes of a theatre rather than illustrations of revealed religion. Demons being hurled downwards, and their shadows painted on the cornices, and, by various artifices, made to form part of the buildings, is illegitimate trickery, and betrays a vulgar aim to deceive the ignorant that is quite beneath the painter of history. Before Michael Angelo and Raffaelle, art was comparatively meagre and puerile; after them it went beyond "the modesty of nature." The first early school wanted knowledge; in the later, knowledge was desecrated. Poverty prevented the one from merging into irregularity; plenty turned to repletion in the other.

An artist who would be great in mural pictorial design, must not be allured from genuine art by the prejudices of the times in which he lives. A petty style of decoration may minister to the caprice of a passing fashion, but it would ill accord with the nervous and masterly mode of fresco painting.

CHAPTER VIII.

ON CONDUCTING LARGE WORKS IN FRESCO.

In beginning large mural decorations, the first step is to paint in all the ornament, it being easier to harmonize subject to ornament than ornament to subject; and arabesques form an excellent key for the tone and colour of the historical painter.

This part completed, it is a good plan to fix the blank cartoons in their respective situations, and then sketch in the general design, as a better judgment can be formed of it when up.

When all the cartoons are painted al rosso di uovo (which very much resembles the appearance of fresco), they should again be placed on the panels, when the full effect of the whole will be seen, which is especially necessary when different hands are employed. Alterations and improvements can then be suggested, and the various cartoons harmonized to suit each other. A work of this kind must of necessity be conducted by one person, who can direct and preserve the unity, though all might execute their own designs, as in the Farnese decorations, where Annibal Caracci, assisted by Agostino and Ludovico, as well as Guido and Domenichino, has nevertheless succeeded in obtaining great harmony with variety.

When the plan is fully arranged, and the panels prepared to all but the last layer of stucco by the plasterer, the painter may commence thus: a portion of the cartoon, suppose it to be a head, must be cut out, and the back of the outline, blackened with charcoal, laid upon the piece of fresh plaster; a point having been passed over the outline, an impression will remain on the stucco.* It is necessary to go speedily over the work with the colour, letting the brush feel the lime, while the pigments incorporate themselves with the ground. Painting for some time on one place, and leaving the stucco untouched in another, is apt to cause inequalities; besides which, in a short space of time it becomes too dry to take the colour well. This being attended to, the paint (worked in an impasto) proceeds delightfully.

Semi-opaque tints, scumbled over solid colour, become very brilliant; the high lights should then

* This is the usual method, but having practised both, I very much prefer the pounce, as described in the chapter on Tempera.

be touched on. The whole to be kept low in tone, as the colour dries considerably lighter. Over the first layer of colour the touches are almost invisible for some seconds.

Dark colours, if first used with white, should be glazed purely afterwards.

Water sprinkled with a long soft brush on the stucco occasionally, will prevent its getting dry too soon.

Flesh should be painted at one time, drapery at another, and always so as to avoid seams in the lights, and where it would be difficult to unite the next part.*

Back-grounds, particularly skies of a large size, must be painted by two or three persons, the superintending artist directing and harmonizing, which he can better see to do than those employed on an individual part. If care is taken to follow the coloured cartoon exactly, no time will be lost in making alterations; and fresco requires all the diligence and judgment possible to conduct it safely and successfully, as there is no touching upon the stucco when dry. Many of the early painters did so, but it turns black, and is very detrimental. There are

* In the frescoes of Raffaelle there are no inequalities; the impasto helps the forms, and proves the knowledge and certainty of his touch.

some modern frescoes in the Vatican where the high lights have all become black from after-touching.

The palette for fresco should be either of porcelain or tin; the ordinary wooden ones soon warp and break, unless long used previously for oil painting.

The brushes must be of hog's hair, both flat and round. Sables are useless, as they soon lose their elasticity.

In the course of drying, fresco exhibits rather an alarming appearance; the colour looks patchy and faint, and a white mould rises to the surface; within two or three months various changes succeed each other, till the picture almost entirely disappears;* gradually, however, as the plaster dries, it re-assumes, with additional beauty, its solidity and clearness.

Michael Angelo was so troubled at the obliterations and disfigurements in the ceiling of the Sixtine Chapel, that, in disgust, he proceeded to the Pope, and begged to resign the work. The latter referred him to Juliano da San Gallo, who explained the phenomenon, and Michael Angelo had soon the satisfaction of seeing his figures restored to more than their pristine excellence.

* This is not always the case, but depends on the nature of the stucco. I have painted fresco upon grounds that present none of these unpleasant appearances, and have dried in the course of a fortnight.

CHAPTER IX.

ON COLOURS USED IN FRESCO.

Few pigments are used in fresco painting, and those principally earths. Mineral, animal, and vegetable substances are destroyed in a short time by the action of the lime.

The following may be used with certainty:—

WHITE.

Calcined Marble, or Stone Lime.

YELLOWS.

Naples Yellow.
Yellow Ochre.
Roman Ochre.
Brown Ochre.
Raw Sienna.
Burnt Sienna.

BLUES.

Ultramarine.*
Ultramarine Ashes.
French Ultramarine.
Cobalt.
Royal Smalt.

BROWNS.

Raw Umber.
Burnt Umber.
Vandyke Brown.
Cologne Earth.

REDS.

Chinese Vermilion, or Native Cinnabar.
Light Red.
Indian Red.
Burnt Copperas.

GREEN.

Terra Verte.

BLACKS.

Ivory Black and Charcoal.

* As a simple test for genuine Ultramarine does not seem

Smalts of various colours, as used for glass painting, are valuable. The colours should be finely ground in water, kept in earthenware cups, and arranged in order in the divisions of a box, with light pigments first, and so on in their gradations.

For flesh tints, use …	Light Red and Lime. Vermilion and White.
For high lights………	Burnt Sienna, varied with Naples Yellow, or Raw Sienna.
For greys……………	Ultramarine Ash and White.

Black, Indian Red, Burnt Sienna, and white (mixed) make good shadows for flesh, as does also Raw Umber, when the subject is very large. Burnt Umber possesses great depth in fresco, and is an excellent colour for the darker shadows.

Draperies, if painted with black and white, may frequently have the lights glazed, which gives a fine effect.

For example, to paint a piece of blue drapery :—Lay it in with black and white, and afterwards glaze with Ultramarine. This will be far more brilliant than if painted solidly with the latter.

Simplicity cannot be too much observed in the colouring as well as in the design.

generally known, the following may be found useful :—If the colour, ground up stiffly with nut oil, begins, after a few hours, to liquify and spread on the palette, it is factitious : if, on the contrary, it remains firmly in a mass, the same as when first mixed, it is genuine lapis lazuli.

CHAPTER X.

I SHALL now proceed to mention the materials of the stuccoes for fresco, beginning with the Greek method according to Vitruvius, and nearly in his words.

LIME.

Lime for the plastering is made of stone or marble (as the Trevertino). It should be slaked long before being used, so that parts not sufficiently calcined may have time to dissolve and be reduced to a proper consistency; for should the lime be fresh or not thoroughly slaked, it will emit pustules, and destroy the surface of the stucco.* To ascertain when it is fit for use, cut it with an axe; if it comes in contact with lumps, the lime is not well tempered —if the iron comes out dry and clean, it is perishing

* The Greek plasterers were very particular in tempering their mortar, considering it as highly essential to the solidity of the work. The arenatum was tempered in a pit, the lime and sand being compounded by men with wooden rammers till thoroughly amalgamated. The same method was adopted with the trullisatio.

and weak, but when fat and well macerated, it will adhere to the iron like glue.

SAND.

River-sand only must be used for fresco on account of its meagreness and not causing fermentation, like pit-sand when in conjunction with lime. Sea-sand is also to be avoided, as the salt exuding from it dissolves the plastering.

POZZOLANA.

Pozzolana is a red earth (found at Puteoli),* and a strong cement, which sets immediately when mixed with water. It renders brick-work exceedingly firm and durable. What we call Roman cement is an imitation of Pozzolana, and possesses many of its qualities.

MARBLE DUST.

This is chippings of marble pounded and sifted into three qualities, the first being a very fine powder.

* From whence it derives its ancient name, Pulvis puteolanea.

ON STUCCOING WALLS.

First process.—Trullisatio, or rough plaster.

The wall or brick-work is to be coated with trowelled plaster, composed of rough sand, pounded brick and tile, and lime, in the following proportions :—

1 part lime.
2 parts river-sand.
1 part pounded brick and tile.

Second process.—Arenatum, or sand-mortar.

Not less than three successive coats of this mortar must be laid over the rough plaster, and each while the preceding one is damp. The more substantial this mortar is, the more durable and solid will be the stucco.

Proportions :—

1 part lime.
2 parts river-sand.

Third process.—Marmoratum, or marble-mortar.

This last process is with lime and marble-dust, of different degrees of fineness, laid on in three successive coats, using the coarsest first. This must be so tempered, as in working not to adhere to the trowel, but to leave it clean and free from mortar.

With the marmoratum, time should be allowed for the first and second coats to dry, before the last is put on.

Proportions :—

1 part lime.

2 parts marble-dust.

Thus, with one layer of trullisatio, three of arenatum, and three of marmoratum, neither fissures nor other defects can appear; and on a solid, well-worked stucco the colours will appear resplendent, and unite together in the stucco, so as to become an incorporated substance, not likely to scale off by age or discharge its colour by cleaning.

If, in lieu of the above, only one layer of arenatum and one of marmoratum are put on over the trullisatio, the colours will not have their proper brilliancy, the plaster will be liable to crack, and the whole, after a time, will decay.

A well-prepared stucco, if required, may be beautifully polished, as was often done by the Greeks.*

* This is an excellent mode for corridors and lobbies, as the surface can be easily washed with a sponge, but it should be employed only upon plain walls. Subjects and arabesques are greatly injured by such a process; it is, in fact, destructive to their artistic character.

CHAPTER XI.

ON ITALIAN STUCCOES, AS USED IN THE FIFTEENTH CENTURY.

IT appears from Vasari that pozzolana was generally adopted with Trevertino lime, both being in high estimation at that period. Good Roman cement and stone-lime I have found to answer nearly as well, it being a firm basis to work upon, and the impasto of colour appearing with greater solidity and brilliancy than on the arenatum, which was used by some later Italian painters.

The effect and force of colour in the frescoes of the Vatican are admirable, yet a preference must decidedly be given to the stucco of the Greeks and Romans.

In examining the remains of the Baths of Titus, I found the stucco, which was about an inch and a quarter in thickness, of the hardness of marble, and greatly superior to that in the Vatican, which, in some instances, is cracking.

Marmoratum was occasionally used where a white

ground was required, as in painting arabesques on ceilings.

Proportions of the three kinds of stucco employed by the Italians:—

POZZOLANIUM.

2 parts lime.

1 part pozzolana, or Roman cement.

MARMORATUM.

2 parts lime.

1 part marble-dust.

ARENATUM.

2 parts lime.

1 part river-sand.

The rough plaster was always pozzolana, lime, and sand.

The Author has lately painted some frescoes upon an improved stucco, or cement, prepared by Messrs. Benson and Logan, the underground of which possesses the properties of the pozzolana, from its hardness and imperviousness to damp, and the last layer seems to resemble, in the course of drying, the marmoratum of the Greeks.

This cement has been adopted, and used successfully for ornamental works, in the firm of Mr. Simpson, in the Strand.

www.ingramcontent.com/pod-product-compliance
Lightning Source LLC
Chambersburg PA
CBHW020930180526
45163CB00007B/2957

* 9 7 8 1 5 2 8 7 1 0 0 3 9 *